D1451007

Johs B. Thue

The Nærøyfjord

SKALD 2006

Map over the Nærøyfjord

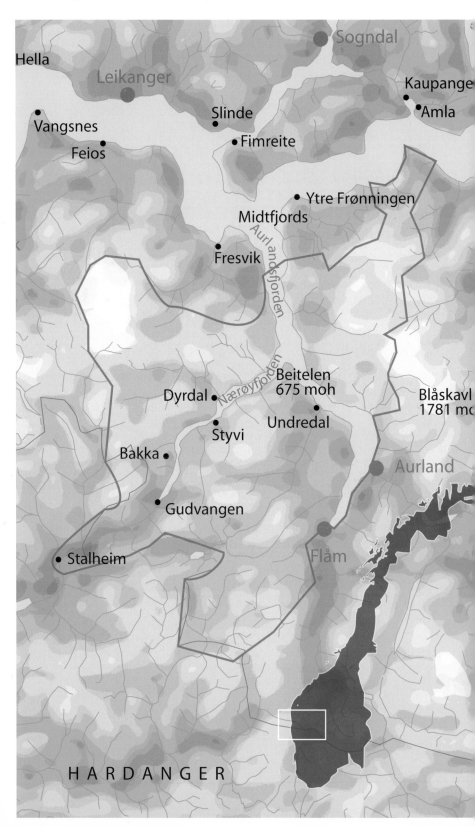

Sogndal

Hella

Leikanger

Kaupange

Slinde

Amla

Vangsnes

Fimreite

Feios

Ytre Frønningen

Midtfjords

Fresvik

Aurlandsfjorden

Nærøyfjorden

Beitelen
675 moh

Dyrdal

Blåskavl
1781 mo

Undredal

Styvi

Bakka

Aurland

Gudvangen

Stalheim

Flåm

H A R D A N G E R

Contents

By the fjord

A rowboat rocks gently up and down as it is anchored up in a cove in the Nærøyfjord. People live here. Nobody can have left his boat or gone away as long as it is tied to a buoy and with a rope attached to land. Without a boat a cove is naked, like a window without curtains. The intimate laps of fjord and seawater rippling along the side of the boat are the timeless conversations between the living and the dead which make our everyday life rich and blessed. Patient small tugs in the land rope tell us of mild forces standing above people. These tugs are nourished by breakers and undercurrents as greetings from the ocean far away, and from the breath of winds. Gentle coves are caressed by mild water, the broken forces, and with a dangerous surge that speaks a language of its own.

Ribbons of dark golden seaweed sway lazily on the surface of the fjord, turning towards the sun like their flower sisters on land. Thousands of rustling small shells cling onto ropes and quay piles. An eel glides along the shoreline, just returned home from the whirling and restless Saragossa Sea. A salmon tries hard to get rid of the salmon lice on its silvery body. A flounder scuttles across the sandy bottom, and a Norway lobster crawls sideways.

Seagulls glide effortlessly between the seashore and the steep crag, following a ferryboat or a ship, then seek restlessly out to the quietest layer of air. The air is divided into layers of quiet emptiness. The treacherous fall-wind is in the air. The seagulls rise vertically to the falling wind and are tossed and shaken, before their wings once again can catch the wind and sail out towards dangers they cannot do without, always searching for food. The rowboat rocks and tugs on the rope, and the buoy disappears.

The Nærøyfjord
– a world heritage site

Give them back something of their natural life.
What they are missing,
but what everybody consciously or unconsciously
is longing for
and their outlook on life will be healthier
and their joy of life will be brighter.

(translated from Fridtjof Nansen)

The British fjord swimmer Lewis Gordon Pugh swam the whole length of the Nærøyfjord in two days in connection with the inscription of the fjord on the UNESCO World Heritage List in the spring of 2003.

Fridtjof Nansen (1861-1930) is one of the best-known Norwegians. He was an Arctic explorer and researcher, oceanographer, zoologist, and diplomat. In addition, he taught the young Norwegian royal family in the early 20th century to become true Norwegians and to love outdoor life, on foot and on skis, summer and winter. In March 1884, only 23 years old, he was travelling from Bergen to Oslo. He followed the thousand-year-old itinerary by way of Voss, down the steep descent of Stalheimskleivi to Gudvangen, and then by boat on the Nærøyfjord to Lærdal. Gudvangen and Lærdal were the key places on the road between the west coast and the inland areas, between the old towns of Oslo and Bergen. Writing about his journey, Nansen says that an immense snow avalanche had blasted across the Nærøyfjord just seconds after the boat passed. This can happen on the Nærøyfjord today as well. Tremendous forces rage. The fjord is narrow and wild. The U-shaped profile shows how the fjord was formed by

Map of "Western Norwegian fjord landscape" showing the protected fjord of the Nærøyfjord.

The Nærøyfjord cuts into the landscape past narrow points jutting out from the steep mountainsides.

glacial erosion in the Quaternary Period (the past one-and-a-half million years up to the present).

Today the Nærøyfjord has become something much more than a travelling stage between east and west. After a UNESCO decision, in the far-off South-African city of Durban, the Nærøyfjord was inscribed on the prestigious World Heritage List in 2005, which includes the most unique natural and cultural monument sites worthy of preservation in the world today. The landscape surrounding the fjord is also included so the area covers more than 709 square kilometres in the municipalities of Aurland, Voss, Vik, and Lærdal. The following passage is taken from one of the criteria used for justifying the inscription on the prestigious list of the Nærøyfjord and also the Geirangerfjord in the county of Møre og Romsdal:

"Their outstanding natural beauty is derived from their narrow and steep-sided crystalline rock walls that rise up to 1400 m direct from the Norwegian Sea and extend 500 m below sea level. Along the sheer walls of the fjords are numerous waterfalls while free-flowing rivers rise up through deciduous and coniferous forest to glacial lakes, glaciers and rugged mountains. There is a great range of supporting natural phenomena, both terrestrial and marine such as submarine moraines and marine mammals. Remnants of old and now mostly abandoned transhumant farms add a cultural aspect to the dramatic natural landscape that complements and adds human interest to the area."

The World Heritage decision was the result of a long process. 15 international experts in various fields gave their assessments. The decision means that the natural and environmental values in Norwegian fjord landscapes are made visible and ensured. This, then, is clear: The Nærøyfjord is among the wildest and most spectacular fjords in the world.

On the present World Heritage List there are 788 monuments and geographical areas in all. Of these there are 154 natural areas. The West-Norwegian fjord landscape has joined a highly outstanding company with world attractions such as the Egyptian pyramids, the Victoria Falls in the south of Africa, the Chinese Wall, and Grand Canyon. From before Norway had five sites on the World Heritage List: Bryggen, the Old Hanseatic Quarter of Bergen; the Urnes Stave Church; The Røros Mining Town; The Rock Drawings of Alta; The Vega Archipelago. The West-Norwegian fjord landscape is the first area to comply with all the natural criteria.

The Nærøyfjord and its surrounding landscape that makes up the World Heritage site is also characterized by cultural diversity. Along the Nærøyfjord – named after the old Norse god Njord – we come across an industrial culture that puts itself within the inner Sogn area in terms of production methods and the use of implements and tools. This fjord branch, including Gudvangen and Stalheim further up the valley, has been a favourite destination for tourists since the late 19th century. All the artists from the national-romantic period came to this area, partly because it was the main thoroughfare between west and east. The fact that the countryside is scenic is also an important element in the prevailing view of nature today. For this reason, close to 300 000 persons from all around the world choose to include the Nærøyfjord on their itinerary.

Tourists from all corners of the world come to see and experience the Nærøyfjord.

Chapter 2

In from the Sea

The brook has withdrawn its branches into the brown mouldy slope
where all the beetles sleep
the greenest of trees are boxing against a blue sky on the hilltops
rapid water
cascading down eight levels
polishing rocks
until Silurian shines
until Cambrium murmurs
water
flowing so thinly across the brown slab barely
into sunlight and mould light

Translated from Kjartan Hatløy: "Riket er ditt, damti,damti". (2005)

The Sognefjord

From Hermansverk, the county capital, you can see how the main Sognefjord splits into fjord branches.

The Sognefjord is the longest and deepest fjord in Scandinavia. The fjord turns and wiggles its way about 170 kilometres into the landmass. By following the fjord to its head, you have come to the centre of Norway. On the map the fjord looks like a tree, like an old oak. The western part is the lower part of the trunk. Further inland, it spreads its branches as in the Nærøyfjord, the Aurlandsfjord, and the Fjærlandsfjord. Mountains, plateaus and hills encircle the fjord. The mountainsides are frequently precipitous all the way down to the fjord surface. From Årdal in the east the fjord becomes gradually deeper westwards, or "out" as they say in Sogn. From Åkrestrand and Vikum, with 1308 metres as its maximum depth, the troughs rise rapidly in uphill steps. At the fjord's westernmost point there is a marked bedrock threshold where the depth varies between 100 and 200 metres.

The name Sogn is derived from "soget" which is a foamy surge or whirlpool. The Gulf Stream and the sun are our two life-giving forces. Where the warm Gulf Stream meets the southbound cold ocean currents from the Norwegian Sea, huge whirlpool currents help to circulate bottom water up to the surface. Thus it is the mixture of water from the cold north and the warm south that has created the name of Sogn. Sogn,

12

or derivations of Sogn, such as Sygnefest or Sygneskard, we find all the way from the Atlantic coastline, and we come across the name in the border areas towards Sunnfjord, Hordaland, and the valley of Gudbrandsdalen. People who live here are "sogningar", whether they are fishermen on the westernmost islands of Solund, mountain farmers in Borgund, or inhabitants at the fjord heads like Flåm and Gudvangen.

The word fjord belongs to the old Norse vocabulary. Fjord as a geographical term gave name to large areas. The word was taken abroad and used on sea lanes cutting into the landscape when Norwegians ruled over the great North Sea empire in the Middle Ages. "Fjordr" has derivations like "Fyrde" and "Firda". The Firda county was the name given to the area north of the Sognefjord when the ancient judicial assembly called "Gulatinget" convened a thousand years ago. In the regions we today call Sunnfjord and Nordfjord, there are a number of fjords, eight of them in Sunnfjord alone.

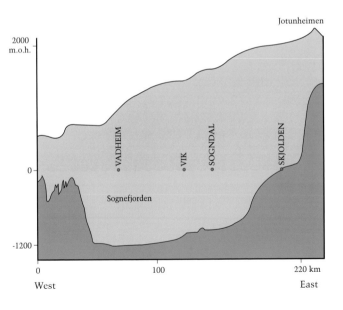

At certain places the fjord depth matches the height of the surrounding mountains.

Winter cruise

It is January. The light is about to break through and give us another new day. We are on our way, in our own boat across the Sognefjord from the county seat of Leikanger. The frost mist on the fjord increases, the air thickens with fog and clouds rolling in from the ocean and the main fjord. All of a sudden it starts to snow, a fine and silent sprinkle of snow falling softly hour by hour, swathing the land in a linen coat. Snow falls on the fjord, on the seashore, in the hillsides, on heather and moss.

Houses disappear. Only a muffled silence remains.

We see the village of Fresvik on our port side and the fjord and the land further east. Above us are hills and mountains. The mountainsides show traces and scars after enormous rain storms. The fan-shaped screes and avalanche tracks have been polished and cleaned. The Earth, our mother, repairs itself. We see the tall and slim juniper trees on the point of Simleneset, where the buoys from the blue mussel facility rock gently on the fjord. On the cultivated fields we see the straight lines of the raspberry plants.

The hamlet of Bakka in 14
winter.

Frønningen and the artist Knut Rumohr

Ahead we see Frønningen which is one of the few manors in western Norway. It has been a private property for centuries. The well-known Lem family owned the manor from 1650 to 1869, when Jan Rumohr bought it. He tore down the old residence and built a new one as we see it today.

Nyborg is located in the hill above Frønningen.

The artist Knut Rumohr (1916-2002) grew up at this place. Later in life he settled down in Oslo, but every summer he returned to his studio at Frønningen. Rumohr is said to be one of the foremost non-figurative Norwegian painters in the 20th century. He alternated between graphic art and painting. The landscape was a central motif in his 60-year-long artistic period. In addition, he was inspired by rural culture and folklore, and he was also a keen collector. Today there are seven buildings surrounding his elegant residence.

Nyborg was Rumohr's retreat. At the hamlet of Åsen, high up above Frønningen, there is a cluster of houses such as dwellings, a barn, and a storage house. Åsen used to be – and still is – a community of its own. They had their own school, and the road zigzags between the holdings. In a period during the Second World War, Rumohr walked about in the mountains and forests of Frønningen, painting small landscapes on plates of bookbinder cardboard. He turned his back to the motif, interpreted it freely, cutting out all unnecessary elements. The artistic expression

15

meant most. An oil canvas from Knut Rumohr's hand in 1941 is entitled "High mountains". We can find reflections of Nyborg and the mountains in the background in the painting.

"Autumn sun" Rumohr has called one of his paintings, made in 1995. Yellow or a reddish orange can be seen under the dark colours, "sometimes scratched to the surface as scars or sparks. A surge of blue amplifies the dark. The sun shines in yellow in the background", writes the art professor Halvdan Ljøsne about this fantastic work of art.

Frønningen with Åsen and the mountain of Bleia as a backdrop.

The elegant residence of the manor at Frønningen.

The Aurlandsfjord

At the point of Simleneset the Aurlandsfjord opens up, shooting into the landmass before splitting up at Beitelen to create a fjord basin. We pay close attention to the draft, landscape and terrain. Up in the sky a pair of eagles chase further into the fjord. A cormorant perches on an iron pole that marks a submerged reef created by rock slides. Man has left its traces everywhere. They needed to put names on places in order to be accurate when looking for sheep or goats, or when attaching a buoy to mark where the whiting was – the chicken of the fjord.

This is where we find the point of Kobbeneset which got its name from "kobbe" (seal), which is often blamed for depleting the fish stocks in the fjord. The otter has also given name to a place. Elsewhere we find place names linked to bears, goats, other animals and trees. Man, tree, animal. But superstition also played a role in giving names to places, such as "Trollagjelet" (the troll's gully), the scariest place along the fjord. This is what the trolls looked like, without a single beautiful feature, merely creepiness, loose rocks and rotten teeth. In the middle of the gully the water has turned to ice. No ice castle exactly, rather a small hell, steep and slippery. The trolls took a liking to this place, in the old imaginary world of myths and legends.

From the basin at Beitelen, we see the built-up area of Aurland, which has an illustrious history from our Norwegian Middle Ages. Aurland was the seat of mighty chieftains who

The car-ferry Skagastøl plying the calm waters of the Aurlandsfjord.

17

Below us is the farm of Stigen on a ledge in the mountainside. Behind the farm we see the forest and the mountains with their valuable resources.

made the whole of Europe their domain. In graves in Aurland we have found Celtic objects, mostly cast bronze objects or parts of them. We can imagine that young boys from Aurland on raids in the western isles tore apart church objects, volumes of books, and harness. These broken bits and pieces became souvenirs from the young people's lives in the west and were brought home as gifts for their girlfriends. The ripples from the Irish Sea reached the Aurlandsfjord. Bjørn Brynjulfson of the mighty Aurland family

had by brute force abducted a high-born woman from Fjordane, Tora Roaldsdatter. He wanted her. After this abduction he found it wise to leave the country with Tora in the same ship. He asked his father for a longship. The father stubbornly refused, but instead he gave him a full-laden merchant ship, throwing these words at his son: "Sail south to Dublin. That will be your best choice". This happened in the 10th century.

"Mid-fjord"

Just to the north of Beitelen we find the stop called "Mid-fjord". It has been said half jokingly that the places in Norway that are best known in Japan are Flåm and "Mid-fjord". At this latter stop boats and ferries meet and connect out on the open sea. If you arrive by express boat from Bergen on your way to Flåm, you can change boats and step onboard the ferry bound for the Nærøyfjord and Gudvangen. Formerly, up to five boats could

meet and connect there. Worried tourists watched their suitcases being flung from one boat to another. It has even been said that husband and wife have become separated from each other by this highly unusual transfer of passengers. The husband landed in Flåm whereas his wife ended up at Gudvangen. Can a couple get a better travel experience than this? The husband in Flåm. The wife at Gudvangen.

Beitelen

The mountain of Beitelen forms the entrance portal both to the Aurlandsfjord and to the Nærøyfjord.

At the vertical cliff of Beitelen the two fjords of Aurlandsfjord and Nærøyfjord separate and head off in two directions. We are now in the midst of an immense mountain plateau, cleaved by the two fjords with wild and narrow side valleys up from the green seashore. At the head of the Aurlandsfjord we find Flåm. Gudvangen marks the head of the Nærøyfjord. Both places are famous tourist destinations. High above the fjords we find the vast mountain plateaus which formed the basis for hunting and fishing, the oldest industries in our country. Up there were also the mountain pastures and the mountain farms which have been a goldmine for farmers in the inner part of Sogn.

The mountain of Beitelen rises dramatically up from the blue fjord, forming an entrance portal to the Nærøyfjord. The old Norse word "beitel" can be translated as chisel in a more modern terminology. A chisel is a wedge-like hand tool to cut or shape wood, stone or metal. The chisel is held at an angle to the material to be shaped and hammered down by rhythmic blows. The mountain of Beitelen looks like a gigantic chisel, slightly angled and ready to cut and shape the landscape and the terrain. The place name of Beitelen most likely belongs to the world of myths as to how terrain and landscape were formed by super-human forces. With such an excellent cutting and shaping tool in the hands of trolls and giants, the whole of the Nærøyfjord and the valley beyond Gudvangen become a narrow wedge, a narrow fjord and a narrow valley.

From the farm of Stigen with a view towards the Aurlandsfjord.

22

The farm of Stigen

Just to the south of the majestic Beitelen is the farm Stigen (literally: the Ladder). In our modern age people have often wondered how it was possible for someone to live at such a place. The ascent to the farm was so steep and impassable that ladders had to be used in order to get past slippery polished rocks. According to anecdotes, these ladders were pulled up to prevent the tax collector from climbing up to the farm. This is a good yarn without any historical foundation. The people at Stigen paid their taxes just like everybody else. However, it was possible to eke out a living on the farm due to the outlying fields and the mountain pastures which provided fodder for their cattle. Butter was the all-important product for the farmer.

The farmyard at Stigen.

The Nærøyfjord

The Nærøyfjord stretches about 18 kilometres to the southwest with a width varying between 300 and 1000 metres. When we observe the Nærøyfjord from a boat or ship, we must bear in mind that nobody lives on the farms for long periods of the year. Just east of Styvi there is a place called "Solaløysa" (literally: a place with no sun). This place could not simply go by any other name, because regardless of season and the sun's position in the sky, the high mountains always block the sunrays from reaching down to this spot. Still, the damp soil and the indirect heat from the mountainsides have made this place green and lush.

We count six avalanche gullies in the course of a few hundred metres. Building electricity and telephone lines here would be pointless. The avalanches would have swept poles and lines out on the fjord. Consequently, there are sea cables from Gudvangen to the hamlets of Bakka, Dyrdal, and Styvi. Dyrdal had a hydroelectric power station of its own from 1923.

The Styvi farm has sought shelter there under the precipitous mountainside. Styvi used to be a sizable farm with two holdings and some crofter's farms. Then we take a look at Dyrdal across the fjord, which has got its name after animal names like reindeer and deer which provided the hunter with food and income. Dyrdal once had a population of 60. In the olden days the place was an administrative centre, then called Ådnehus with a court and an inn. In 1805, these functions were transferred to Gudvangen. The houses at Dyrdal are big, bearing testimony to prosperity and economic success, but the age of prosperity in the villages is a thing of the past. It was actually Mother Nature herself that put an end to it all. The last small field was cultivated, the leaves for fodder were removed from the outlying fields, the last mountain farm deserted. There was nothing left to eke out. Then the seam unravelled like the seam of a silk stocking. The holes grew bigger and bigger. Eventually the last people gave up. In the past decade up to 2004, Nærøy was one of the rural areas in the county of Sogn og Fjordane that lost most people. Today there are about 100 persons living in the church "sokns" (subdivisions of a parish). But today we must go all the way to Bakka, with a population of 18, before we can find someone to talk to during the long winter months.

View from the mountain of Skjerpisnuten towards the Nærøyfjord.

Unreliable ice

The Nærøyfjord can easily freeze over because the water is almost fresh. The ice-covered fjord has caused communication problems throughout the years.

We are in the midst of the Norwegian avalanche country. In the Nærøyfjord, avalanches cross the fjord at several places. In winters with much snow, these avalanches regularly blast down the mountainsides, especially in spring. According to what older people say, it is the "powder avalanches" consisting of loose, dry new-fallen snow that are most dangerous. On his journey on the Nærøyfjord in March, 1884, Fridtjof Nansen was told that a boat had almost been hit by an avalanche. People on the boat fortunately heard the sound of the avalanche crashing down the mountainside. They set full speed ahead to get clear of the enormous snow masses. They squeaked through, but the stern was filled with snow almost to the entrance down to the cabin. In the wink of an eye, the whole fjord behind the boat was filled with snow.

The fjord ice in the innermost part of the Nærøyfjord and other fjords for that matter is highly unreliable. It led to cancellation of church services and thus exemption from listening to condemnations and admonitions on the part of vicars. The Norwegian word for this type of ice is "mein-is" and we find references to this in a number of topographical descriptions, bishops' reports, and in land registers. The unreliability of this ice meant that special ice boats were constructed, both at Flåm and at Styvi. At the Fjord Museum at Kaupanger we find a small boat of this type, looking a little lost among the stately and elegant features of the other local boats from Sogn. This small and rather unusual boat is the ice boat from Flåm, built as a flat-bottomed rowboat

26

with runners attached underneath. The boat came to the museum from Flåm in 1913, and in the catalogue for the boat we can read: "Previously much used to navigate the fjord from Aurland to Flåm when the ice was unsafe". A similar boat still exists today at Styvi, privately owned by Botolv Hov.

The foremost boat expert in Norway, Bernhard Færøyvik from Solund, took measurements of this boat and came to the conclusion that it must have been built about 1860, but that this type of boat was much older – "several hundred years". The boat has a sail thwart, and, according to Færøyvik's notes, the boat had a square sail. What distinguishes this boat from other flat-bottomed rowboats are two solid runners under the bottom, as well as solid iron plates on the front part of the bottom. Another boat expert, Arne Emil Christensen Jr. has later questioned Færøyvik's conclusions as to the age of this boat type. He thinks that the boat is a typical cultural loan from eastern Norway, and that the ice boat is an old phenomenon in Europe, especially in the Netherlands, both as a practical means of transport and as a leisure boat. What is important in this respect is the fact that this ice boat played an important part in ensuring safe transportation between villages, but also as an important link in travelling longer distances, between Oslo and Bergen.

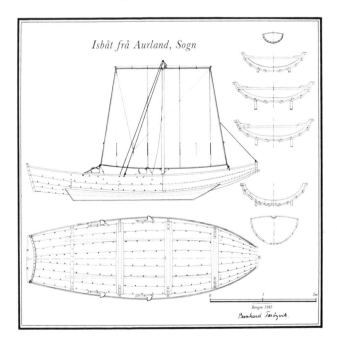

Isbåt frå Aurland, Sogn

Bergen 1943
Bernhard Færøyvik.

Drawing of a so-called ice-boat from Flåm. This boat is on display at the Fjord Museum at Kaupanger (De Heibergske Samlinger – Sogn Folkemuseum).

Bakka

Bakka.

The village of Bakka with its old cluster of houses still almost intact lies ahead. The mountain of Bakkanosi rises 1400 metres up towards the sky. The mountain of Vindeggi a hundred metres lower. Further into the fjord, about eight kilometres from Bakka, is Gudvangen.

We go ashore at Bakka. The old school building, now without any pupils, blackboard, chalk or hymns, is located close to the seaside. Close by is a big warehouse with stone walls reminiscent of the old Viking houses, which consisted mostly of stone. The slaves were always carrying stones.

The population exploded in these villages in the mid 19th century. All possible fields were cultivated. Crofters carried soil in wooden buckets in the spring evenings. Women prayed to God for a better existence, but their prayers were seldom heard. They left, to America once they had enough money to pay for the tickets. As long as the population was sparse, people accepted that they had to go all the way to Undredal for church services, baptism, confirmation and weddings. Maybe it was also accepted that the coffins had to be transported by rowboat or by ice boat all the way to Aurlandsvangen and be buried in consecrated ground there. But with the population boom, going to church became a too long and cumbersome affair: Corpses to Aurlandsvangen, infants to Undredal. In 1835, a wedding procession was on its way out the fjord to the church at Undredal when they were surprised by a snow avalanche. Ten people lost their lives on the fjord that day. Something had to be done to change this inhumane and unchristian way of getting to church.

As early as in the 1830s, local people brought up the issue of getting their own church and graveyard in the Nærøy "sokn". It was even discussed to move the Undredal church to Nærøy, but nothing came out of it. In the late 1840s, the graveyard was taken into use at Bakka. In 1859, the white-painted church was completed, signifying that the light had entered the fjords, the new light that modernized Norway. The church is still light both outside and inside. This white-painted church is perhaps the most photographed in the whole country. Elegant cruise ships glide slowly through the narrow strait of Bakkasundet practically every day in the summer season. Photos of this church must surely be found in private albums all over the world. The story of the church, on the other hand, belongs to Inner Sogn.

Altar and altarpiece at Bakka church.

We enter the church on a January morning and are pleased to see such a beautiful and well-kept building. The altarpiece is so special that we have rarely seen anything like it. The motif is "Jesus in the Garden of Gethsemane", painted by Nils Bergslien (1853-1928). Jesus looks like a Nordic hero, with sharp features and long, blond hair. He is quite simply the identical twin brother of Fridtjof the Brave in Bergslien's masterful interpretation with his paintbrush. By the way, Bergslien was perhaps the most important painter of Christmas cards in this country. He specialized in painting Father Christmas, portraying him as a chubby character with white hair and beard – a new national symbol. Father Christmas could have come from Voss or Sogn. Nils Bergslien had a creative mind.

The frame of the altarpiece is nearly just as special, and it was carved by Magnus Dagestad (1865-1957). Dagestad was the woodcarver from Voss who was an inspiration to our foremost woodcarvers. Fairly soon, animal ornaments decorated hotel verandas along our fjords. And in Nærøy woodcarvers entered once more the church room in the early 20th century, as they had done it in the High Middle Ages. At the Urnes Stave Church, which is also included in the UNESCO World Heritage List, the knife has carved intricate, ornamental patterns that can still take our breaths away.

Boat connections

*The car-ferry
Gudvangen on the
Nærøyfjord.*

Bakka and Dyrdal were the old ports of call in the Nærøyfjord for the local steamship company of "Fylkesbaatane". Bakka came first with sporadic stops in the 1880s, but it was not until 1899 that Bakka was included in the regular routes of "Lærdal" in the Inner Sogn fjord basin.

People at Dyrdal also wanted to be linked to the modern world with a regular boat connection. In 1906, the residents of Dyrdal

applied for a stop, but only in 1924 did the board of directors of
the steamship company decide that Dyrdal would be included
with a stop once a week in the boat's winter schedule out from
Gudvangen. There was no quay at Dyrdal so the boat had at first
to be boarded out on the fjord. After much hard work on the part
of the residents and other helpers, a new wooden quay filled with
rock was completed in 1926.

Gudvangen

Some cruise ships inch their way all the way in to Gudvangen past the narrow strait at Bakka.

Gudvangen is the meeting-place between fjord and land on the old Royal Postal Road Bergen – Filefjell – Oslo. From Gudvangen, with its sheltered location on the sandy flats by the river delta and with an ancient stone wall in front of the houses as a protection against the violent gusts of wind from the snow avalanches, there has at all times gone a main road to Voss. The road follows the narrow and wild valley of Nærøydalen for about 10 kilometres up to the steep climb of Stalheimskleivi. The Nærøyelva river winds its way down the valley, nourished by water from the rivers of Brandsetelva and Brekkedalselva, as well as Jordalselva from the north. The main river is an excellent salmon and sea trout river.

The history of Gudvangen precedes the Viking Age. At this place there were market stalls that are now being recreated. There the chieftain's woman has treaded lightly about with her maids a respectful distance behind her. They saw white gravel and rocks in the mountainsides. With combs in their hair they felt a life with the wild taste of honey in it. Far out to the west were the waves of the ocean, other lands and countries. But much closer, at Holmo between Styvi and the strait of Bakkasundet, there were huge burial mounds. The mounds of rocks marked distance to other families and generations. They felt the rustling of the tree leaves and believed in the spirit of the trees.

The first human beings, Ask and Embla (Ash and Elm) were made of wood and had soul. Fishermen came to Gudvangen with

their fish, shepherds came down from the mountains with hides and meat. Sometimes a one-eyed falconer could wander about the marketplace with his cage. People were awestruck by his presence. Millstone makers from Åfjorden were there, too. With dust in their hair they carried the vitally important stones ashore from their big rowboat. Then the market was over. Ships and boats were launched when the wind came down the valley and made the start of their outward voyage on the fjord easier. From inside the mountains they could hear the strangely beautiful sound of song and play. The underworld was having a feast deep inside the cold mountain. And all this has been recreated and can be experienced once more during the annual Viking market, and in a cool grotto in the mountain itself.

The history of Gudvangen starts before the Viking Age.

On a mountain ledge at Gudvangen we find the farm Solbjørgane, now deserted. Living at this farm literally became too much of an uphill struggle. This is a good example of what the writer and historian from Sogn, Olav Hoprekstad, meant when he wrote: "Harsher living conditions, heavier and worse working fields and roads than in the valley of Nærøydalen no farmers anywhere else in Sogn have experienced". One of the farms is called Hemri. At this place a large block of rock tumbled down the mountainside and was broken to bits and pieces down in the valley. This is the Hemris-scree, probably the largest rock scree in any valley in the country.

Stalheim and the rise of tourism

The old postal road between east and west became the golden route when tourism developed in the latter part of the 19th century. The 1890s saw a building boom of Norwegian wooden hotels. Beautiful buildings, marked by the new Romantic movement with its highly special architecture, the so-called Swiss style, with spires, arcades, turrets, and animal ornamentation carved in wood. Hotels at Voss, Stalheim, Gudvangen, Flåm and Lærdal were all built in this style.

The old wooden hotel at Stalheim burned down in a dramatic fire in 1959 and 25 persons lost their lives. A new hotel rose out of the ashes. Only a few metres from this hotel we find "Fuglehaugen", the life's work of the hotel owner Kaare Tønneberg. Twenty old buildings, filled with objects from the baroque golden age are located there, but also objects from rococo, and Empire mixed with Norwegian rural art. The name Stalheim may indicate that the place must have ancient traditions as a place of rest for travellers. The Old Norse word "stadall" actually means a place that makes you stop.

At Gudvangen, the "Vikingvang Hotell & Café" was erected during this period, in the Swiss style, of course, with verandas and slate roof. The word element "Gud" in Gudvangen was replaced with Viking, thus Vikingvang. This is a reflection of our own historical golden age, the Viking Age, which the hotel owner thought would have a better international marketing appeal than "Gud" (God). The hotel community at Gudvangen was in fact ahead of its time. It was not until a hundred years later that the Viking name started to be used extensively in the promotion of Norwegian tourism. Maybe this had something to do with the romantic Viking idealism of Kaiser Wilhelm II who since 1889 considered Gudvangen and the Nærøyfjord among his favourite places to visit.

The Fresvik glacier *The Nærøyfjord*

How were fjords made?

If we climb up the steep mountainsides along the fjord, we will be standing on a relatively level plateau. This beautiful and fascinating plateau is a remnant of a much wider plateau that geological processes such as weathering and erosion acted upon up to about 50 million years ago. Then about 50 million years ago, forces beneath the surface of the earth caused the earth's crust to be faulted, tilted, folded, and lifted. Cracks in the crust opened up where the present coastline is. The landmass lifted, and the maximum uplift was in the west, making the land surface tilt to the east. The old land surface was lifted more than 1000 metres above the present sea level.

Then other forces took over. Water cut down in the bedrock. There were many periods of glaciation. The glaciers advanced and receded, eroding the bedrock under the ice, pressing the landmass down by their sheer weight. As the ice gradually melted, the pressure eased and the land once more rose out of the ocean. We find clear evidence of this along the whole length of the Sognefjord. Terraces that once marked the former sea level today lie up to 100 metres higher. At the heads of fjords, rivers deposited enormous deltas. These are now big flat areas that we find high up above the present sea level.

Climate

Western Norway is a region characterized by big contrasts in terms of landscape and climate, from the gentle and smiling to the frightening and harsh. Western Norway consists of bays and coves along a green and winding seashore where people have settled down. At the same time, avalanches crash down the steep mountainsides in the winter months. Highways across the mountain passes may be closed for days on end. Blizzards from the west may knock you off your feet. The forces of Mother Nature can be hard on mankind.

The fjords catch the mild ocean currents from the Mexican Gulf so vital to the climate, making it possible to live so far north. Even in midwinter, it takes long spells of cold weather before the fjords freeze. Above our heads there is a constant struggle between dry, ice-cold air from the Arctic and moist, almost tropical air from the south.

There are substantial differences in terms of climate and weather within this region. The innermost villages that the Nærøyfjord is part of, has very little precipitation. However, we cannot talk about a continental climate as the fjord, with its soft and caressing woman's arms, is too good a temperature regulator. A case in point is the tree line, which in the easternmost parts of the fjord may go up to 1000 metres, but falls down to 200-300 metres once the contact with the fjord disappears.

In addition, we find significant differences in precipitation between the eastern and western parts of the fjord. Air heavy with rain from the ocean releases water when it collides with cold air from the north or when it hits steep mountainsides, rises and cools off. The result is much precipitation along the coast and very little further inland. The average precipitation along the Sognefjord may vary from 2000 millimetres on the coast, about 1000 millimetres in the central part, and down to 400-500 at Lærdal and Aurland.

In the winter there can be heavy snowfalls in the mountains. Grindafleten tourist lodge. The car-ferry at Beitelen (left)

Chapter 2

Nature
and man

Mother Nature can be a generous friend, but it can also be a dangerous adversary that you have to show respect all the year round.
Not a single building has been nailed and timbered, not a field has
been ploughed, not a wall has been built, without people having
used their knowledge and experience of nature's forces. Farms
and houses glide into the landscape where the snow avalanches
sweep past them at close range, with their eerie sounds and kill-
ing blasts of air. The snow drift accumulating in gaps and gullies
is a neighbour feared by people. These snow drifts may lose their
hold with the extremely warm and dry southerly föhn winds that

Sun-dried grass, hay, was the farmer's gold. Here fjord ponies take the hay into the barn.

Juniper berries (lat. Juniperus communis).

prompt new growth in plants and trees. Knowledge concerning the tracks of these avalanches has been handed down from one generation to another as long as people have lived at these places. Nevertheless, even with this knowledge, avalanches have taken lives, many lives. The most dangerous snow avalanche is perhaps "Hestnesa".

In the forest on the hillsides the silver-white trunks and the tiny green leaves of the birches glisten in the May sunshine. The alder and the mountain ash come to life with its red berries so full of pectin and bittersweet taste. The odd pine tree whispers and rustles in the wind. The oak stands guard over our history. It is as old as the hills. And then the ash, the magical tree with its life-giving foliage. The woodland birds coo, the heath cock and hen. The ptarmigan jumps about among the twisted dwarf birch, finding nourishment in swelling buds. Highest up on a ledge sits the eagle, towering like a shadow from the beginning of time over land and terrain. Such is the forest, and such are the mountainsides along the fjord, the Nærøyfjord.

Life along the fjord

For those who wanted to settle down along the fjords, all choices and life directions were decided by the fact that so little land could be cultivated. The narrow strip of land along the sea alone gave very little food and income. People had to look elsewhere, to the fjord, to the hills, and the mountains to supplement their livelihood. In large parts of the country, a characteristic feature of the economic activity was that most of the land area available was only suitable for what we can call extensive harvesting. To an extreme degree we can see this along the Nærøyfjord. Forage plants had to be harvested and stored in the summer to be used during the long winter months. These plants were harvested both below and above the tree line. Cattle, sheep and goats were led up to higher pastures for a couple of months every summer, first in the outlying fields, later on up in the mountains. People followed the animals, looked after them and produced butter, cheese and sour-milk.

There, then, we find copses of birch, hayfields, pastures, as well as areas for producing fodder and foliage. These pollarded trees – where branches have been cut off to encourage new growth – have now been protected in western Norway. The trees are still

Sheep from Dyrdal on their way to the slaughterhouse, transported by tractor and boat.

Old hunting installation (pitfall) at Skammadalshøgdi by the trail between Grindafleten and Undredal.

standing as reminders of this very special production of forage which put so strong demands to access of labour and working hours that it disappeared completely as the Norwegian agriculture was modernized, humanized and made more worth living from the 1950s. The old agriculture was, on the other hand, an interaction, a closely knit web, between man and nature from the fjord, the seashore and all the way up to the high mountains. All farms had boathouses and mountain farms. But there were also barns in the outlying fields, lamb sheds, hayfields, stone fences, piles of rock from clearing the land, and tracks leading up to the pastures and mountain farms in an intricate pattern, where the borders between the properties were marked with a cross in the rock.

However, it was still the case that cultivated land produced most food. The permanent settlement was linked to the most fertile place. The small cultivated field was the foundation, but people also settled down where there were good opportunities for animal husbandry, fishing, as well as various supplementary industries. The result was a settlement pattern where most of the country remained uncultivated and unpopulated.

The area around the Nærøyfjord covers the whole span of the cultural history in the west-Norwegian fjord landscape. Archaeological finds trace this cultural history as far back as the Younger Iron Age. Then there existed a highly developed hunting culture in the mountains and the immediate areas around the Nærøyfjord. From the Iron Age and the Middle Ages a number of big pitfalls, guiding fences, in addition to a series of cairns and built-up positions for using bow and arrow have been registered. The reindeer in the mountains played an important part in getting enough food.

"Potato sogningar"

The inner fjord villages of Sogn went through an enormous population boom in the first half of the 19th century. The main reason was undoubtedly the falling rate of infant mortality. More people grew up. How best to explain this population increase is a strongly debated issue among historians, demographers, and doctors. One thing, though, there seems to be agreement on: Something can be explained by improved nourishment.

In terms of the Inner Sogn area, this can clearly be attributed to the use of potatoes in people's daily fare. Potatoes could

A simple diet and hard physical work has given high life expectancy. Life expectancy for women in the Sogn region is among the highest in the world.

be harvested every year, they were hardy plants, contained C vitamin, and were virtually carbohydrate bombs. In a very short time towards the end of the 18th century, the potato was taken into use in people's daily diet in many ways. We know this dietary change from the formation of new word combinations such as potato flatbread, potato porridge, potato flour, potato dumpling, potato spirits, and as flat potato cake. There was hardly any dish where the potato could not be used. The Inner Sogn was a typical potato area, and the people in this area were nicknamed "potato sogningar". "He is like a potato, and can be used in everything", people said about a person who was a jack of all trades. Besides, in the early 19th century, potatoes became the most important barter commodity for the people of the Inner Sogn area, exchanging it with fish and herring that the coastal people came sailing into the fjords with.

The pale linden tree

One of the most special deciduous trees in western Norway is found along this fjord. This is a rare mutant variety of a linden tree (lime tree) with pale lemon-coloured leaves. The yellow colour is most likely due to a delayed chlorophyll development which is a known phenomenon in other tree species as well, probably caused by a genetic defect.

This pale linden tree - protected as early as in 1933 – lets its leaves rustle softly in the fjord breeze, casting its shadows on the forest floor. Songbirds flutter almost soundlessly from one branch to another. If you take a closer look, you will find a pattern in the bark, with wrinkles as in an old face. Insects live in this bark and in the branches and foliage.

The white wagtail

The white wagtail may serve as an example of the diversity in our fauna and bird life along the Nærøyfjord. Previously, this migrant bird used to come to these shores in May. Now we can observe it in the first days of April. The bird spends the cold winter months along the Mediterranean shores, bobbing her long and slender tail by the pyramids of Egypt, another UNESCO World Heritage Site.

There are few birds in the western Norwegian landscape that have more omens and signs attached to its name than the white wagtail. The first part of the Norwegian word for wagtail – "linerle" – means linen. If the bird was observed high up in the air, this meant that the flax stalks would be long. If it was sitting on the ground, on the other hand, the flax plant would be short. If it sat bobbing on a rock on the seashore, with its tail pointing straight out to the fjord and was looking at you at the same time, this was indeed a bad omen. Then death was imminent, old people said. They always tried to find out where it was the first time it was observed in spring. It would be a good sign if they saw it the first time in a black and newly ploughed field. There it would follow the plough share to pick up worms to regain its strength after the long migratory flight. Then the cornfield would turn yellow and ripen to provide bread in the autumn. If it came with a northwest wind and in a cold snap, they called it a "wagtail spell", in the same way as when they talked about a "cuckoo spell" shortly after its highly recognizable sound echoed in the hillsides. Both these birds brought bad weather with them and were signs of cold weather and snowfall.

The white wagtail builds its nest in the proximity of farm houses and mountain farms. The nest is frequently found in holes or stone walls, lined with dry grass and its own feathers. The eggs are greyish white with dark speckles.

The Royal Postal Road

The old Royal Postal Road at Gudvangen.

There were many natural obstacles for those who wanted to travel long distances in Norway. Deep forests and steep mountains meant that it was hard to travel by land many places. The Nærøyfjord is a detour, but this early developed sea lane was much easier than travelling overland.

In the late age of migration (400-600 AD), iron had made it possible to build bigger, more seaworthy vessels. On the fjords it was possible to row or sail deep into the country. The summer months were the busiest months for travelling, then as it is now. The fjord and the sea also opened up the country to the outside world. Norway became oriented towards the west because of this. The Atlantic orientation started far into the fjords.

When the official postal service was established in Norway in the 1640s, the post between Bergen and Oslo was transported by farmers by way of Voss, down the Staheimskleivi and the valley of Nærøydalen to Gudvangen and Bakka, and then by boat to Lærdal. In 1876, the steamship companies took over the postal service.

From Lærdal the post was carried up to Borgund, then across the mountain pass of Filefjell and down to the valley of Valdres before entering the wide and open landscape close to Oslo. This was the postal route up to 1908. In the summer months the post was transported by boat every day between Bergen and Oslo, at least from the 1840s. It was in fact the need for a safe

The old Royal Postal Road at the hamlet of Styvi.

48

postal service that formed the basis for the modern Norway. The postal routes on steam ships came first. This was the situation everywhere, also along the Sognefjord and around the coast. But on the some days in the summer, and the whole winter season, the post went overland. This service lasted until the Bergen Line, the rail connection between eastern and western Norway was completed in the early 20th century.

On the road down from Stalheim to the valley of Nærøydalen there were places where hanging ladders were used. These were attached to the slippery rock along the river bank. Somewhat safer it was to go by way of "Nåli" (the Needle) as they called it. This meant to go by way of Sivle and then onwards to Stalheim. However, "Nåli" was never completely safe. It is often the case that legends tend to have a pedagogical moral, with strong elements of warnings and admonitions. According to one legend, a horse slid on the slippery surface. The man could not but watch the horse with its packsaddle fall down hundreds of metres to be crushed at the bottom. The man was left with nothing but the bridle in his hands.

It was hardly any better to negotiate the road down from Stalheim to Gudvangen. Up until fairly recent times, people and motorists were understandably afraid of the steep road with its twisting hairpin curves. The road was also exposed to rock slides and snow avalanches. In addition, it was hard to get across the river and big rock screes. Many prayers have been sent from this road to our Almighty God when the rain lashed down and the hot föhn winds struck in February. There cannot have been any other horror road like this in Europe.

The Royal Postal Road that we find again from the farm Styvi is a beautiful cultural monument and a popular road for hikers. The old postal roads speak volumes of the need for connections that were so vital for uniting our country and for developing our trade systems. But these roads are also manifestations of what could not be negotiated by the obstacles Mother Nature has given us.

Road maintenance

There lived so few people in the valley of Nærøydalen and further along the fjord that these farmers alone could not take care of the hard work of maintaining this road. As far back as 1780 at least, farmers from Vangsnes, Leikanger, Feios and Fresvik worked on the main road in Nærøydalen, according to a report from the county governor Tostrup to the County Council in 1849. This was a response to an application from the farmers of Feios to be exempted from road work and maintenance on the road from Gudvangen to the Skjerpe bridge. These farmers wanted the county to be in charge of this work. The situation was actually worse for the farmers further out in the fjord: The farmers from Leikanger and Vangsnes had to maintain their road sections at Stalheimskleivi and at Oppheim in Voss. These duties caused much discontent. The farmers were fined if they did not turn up or did not maintain the roads properly, but they complained, appealed, and cursed the authorities and officials. By a new division of road sections and areas of responsibility, the farmers from the mid-Sogn area were exempted from road work in Nærøydalen when a new Road Act was passed in 1824.

From 1828, these demanding duties were shifted on to the farmers of Aurland. However, these road duties on top of their previous commitments became too much for them. They had also had the responsibility for road maintenance in the valleys of Aurlandsdalen and Flåmsdalen. For this reason, the decision from 1828 that the farmers of the mid-Sogn area would be exempted from working in Nærøydalen was revoked only five years later. This situation continued for many years. The County Council repeatedly renewed the order of extra duties for farmers who lived within 40 kilometres from a road that the state authorities needed. These farmers rarely or never used this road themselves, they wrote. This was correct, as the people from the mid-Sogn area had square-sailed "jekts" and always used boats to go to Bergen or other markets on the open and ice-free Sognefjord.

VED GUDVANGEN, SOGN.　　　　　　　　　　　　　　　　K. KNUDSEN. BERG.

The steamship "Lærdal" – the pearl of the Sognefjord

No local community can be isolated and not be influenced by what is happening around them. The new, modern age for the Nærøyfjord came only with the small, privately owned steamship "Gudvangen". Then came S/S "Lærdal" that the state authorities practically ordered the "Nordre Bergenhus Amt" (the present county of Sogn og Fjordane) to build in order to ensure the postal service in the Inner Sogn area. This was another example of the greater society overriding the local and regional levels for the benefit and advancement for the people. The small steamer

52

"Lærdal" was the first ship that the county built in this country. Besides, "Lærdal" was the first local steamer of the county steamship company. In retrospect, this ship has been looked upon as a vessel both with a soul and an identity of her own, but the ship was scrapped in 1938.

In 1875, the Norwegian Storting (Parliament) demanded that the county should get hold of a boat that could operate the service between Lærdal and Luster, and between Lærdal, Aurland and Gudvangen. From January till August, 1873, the privately owned "Gudvangen" carried post between Lærdal, Luster and Gudvangen. Then the ship was sold to Sweden. But the financial situation for the four ships of the county steamship company, with an almost revolutionary start in 1858, was far from good with heavy debts. In spite of this, the county politicians felt forced to build a smaller ship. "Lærdal" had a deck house aft with a small first class saloon, ticket office, galley and cabins, and a larger first class saloon under deck aft, and second class under the forward deck. The ship started up its regular service in March, 1876, between Lærdal, Luster, Aurland, and Gudvangen, as the Storting had wanted. The ship had boat connection with the ships to and fro Bergen. In August, 1878, the ship ran ashore in the Aurlandsfjord.

In July, 1883, the railway line between Bergen and Voss was opened. This meant that the postal route from Bergen to Lærdal was reorganized in such a way that the post was carried by rail from Bergen to Voss, then overland to Gudvangen, and by boat from Gudvangen to Lærdal. "Lærdal" then went five times a week between Lærdal and Gudvangen. Later on, "Lærdal" was sent north to Nordfjord to be used in a local route up there. However, in 1887, the privately owned "Ørnen" started a regular service between Lærdal, Gudvangen, and Balestrand. The county authorities then returned "Lærdal" to the Sognefjord to get rid of the competitor. "Ørnen", by the way, ran ashore in the Lærdalsfjord in October, 1898, and sank like a stone.

When the Bergen Railway Line was opened for traffic in 1909, it took over much of the post and passenger traffic that used to go by way of Lærdal. The train put an end to the old communication centre in the Inner Sogn area. The small steamship "Lærdal" plied the fjord arms for a long period of time. In the summer months, she carried passengers from all corners of the world, even royalty and other prominent men and women. In the winter months, the local passengers and the post were most important. Then the small steamship had to cope with rotten and thick fjord ice.

Mine, "whitestone" (anorthosite).

The white rock is crushed and is often used as a top layer on paved roads.

The white mountains

When we travel along the Nærøyfjord and in Gudvangen, we notice many places that the mountainsides and screes are coloured white. The reason is that this area has enormous deposits of anorthosite, a rock that can be applied in many interesting ways. It is, therefore, natural that Aurland should have chosen white anorthosite from Gudvangen to be their municipal rock. "NGU" (Geological Survey of Norway) has classified the anorthosite in the Nærøydalen – Mjølfjell area as a national mineral resource. Helge Henriksen, associate professor at the Sogn og Fjordane University College ("HSF"), describes the white mountains in the following way:

"Anorthosite is an igneous rock that has originally solidified deep below the earth's surface from magna especially rich in calcium and aluminium. The rock consists of more than 90% of the light mineral plagioclase feldspar, with a varying content of sodium, calcium, aluminium, and silicon. Depending on the content, the plagioclase may be white, light violet or brownish in colour. In addition, the anorthosite may contain smaller amounts of dark minerals. Anorthosite is an extremely rare rock found in few places in the world, but Norway has enormous deposits of it in the Bergen area, at Egersund, and in the inner area of Sogn and the county of Hordaland."

The characteristic shape of Jordalsnuten has inspired both painters and poets. Its characteristic conical shape is caused by a geological process called exfoliation, whereby flakes of the rock anorthosite peel off like the rings of an onion.

In Sogn and the county of Hordaland, the anorthosite covers an area of some 700 square kilometres, and the deposits are at least two kilometres thick. The anorthosite in Sogn is about 1700 million years old, belonging to detached thick slivers of Precambrian bedrock that were thrust tens of kilometres from the northwest during the formation of the Caledonian mountain range 400 million years ago. In recent years, scientists have found out that the moon consists mostly of 4400-million-year-old anorthosite. Americans call it moon rock.

The Sogn anorthosite contains much calcium and can be easily dissolved even in its natural state. It is this dissolved calcium that gives the soil and freshwater in the Inner Sogn area an extra protection against acidification. On the other hand, the minerals in the anorthosite are poor in potassium and phosphor. Coupled with the high content of aluminium this is not a particularly good combination for the vegetation. In some of the anorthosite areas, we can see polluted spots of anorthosite soil completely free of vegetation. Weathered anorthosite has a characteristic greyish-white / milky-white colour which has led to place names such as Mjølfjell in Voss, and Grånosi in Aurland.

In the valley of Nærøydalen, extraction of white anorthosite has been carried out since 1964. A large part of the production consists of crushed stone. In recent years, large parts of the production have been exported to Sweden as a raw material in mineral wool. The rock has also properties that make it much demanded on the European continent – especially from Germany - as a top surface of asphalt to make it lighter. Black asphalt absorbs light from the car headlights, and it is a relief to drive on a light asphalt on a dark autumn night.

Chapter 3

Mythology
and culture

Snorri Sturluson (1178-1241) was the great chieftain, poet and historian on Iceland in the High Middle Ages. Snorri's Younger (Prose) Edda and the Elder (Poetic) Edda are the most important sources for our knowledge of the Norse mythology. The Norse gods are divided into two groups: the Vanir and the Aesir. Njord, Frey and Freya belonged to the first group. It is their names we come across in this area. Njord has lent his name to this narrow fjord, with the wildest and most dramatic scenery we have in this country.

When we have such strong links between nature and Norse mythology, this is due to the fact that people felt bound to nature. They believed firmly that nature consisted of forces that had to be treated well. Of special importance were the growth and breeding forces in the fields, for animals and people alike. Religion played a particularly important role in the so-called heathen society, that is, the period prior to the year 1000 AD in Norway. Fear of shame and a desire for honour were the most important religious driving forces. People were concerned with ensuring a good reputation after their death. Being proud was a highly desirable quality. Breaches of the moral laws had to be rectified in relation to other people. The pre-Christian cult was based on the idea that even if people were biologically dead, they were not dead in a social sense. The living and the dead belonged to the same community, and through certain rituals it was possible to communicate with the dead. Those who possessed this communication ability, the prophetess (sibyl) and the chieftain, had much power.

The transition from heathendom to Christianity is a major event in Norwegian history. In 1075, the Archbishop Adam of Bremen recorded an eyewitness observation of the great place of worship ("hov") in Uppsala, Sweden. The place was adorned with gold, and people worshipped the idols of Wotan ("Odin"), Thor and Frey. Wotan was the supreme god, god of victory and the dead. He and his wife Freya decided which men would die on the battlefield, and then they split the fallen men among themselves. Thor was the god of the weather and wind, lightning and thunder. Frey and his sister Freya gave health, prosperity and fertility. In Frey's name a woman and a man could sleep together on a field before spreading the seed-corn - "God's loan" – in spring. This ensured a good yield. The corn was God's loan to mankind. Frey gave the dead peace and sensual pleasure in an intimate relationship between woman and man. The idol of Frey contained an enormous breeding organ. At weddings, sacrifices were made to Frey. The Norse mythology had a positive view of body and relationship between woman and man. The idol of Frey contained an enormous breeding organ. At weddings, sacrifices were made to Frey. The Norse mythology had a positive view of body and sexuality. Sexual practice and the biological functions of women such as menstruation, pregnancy and birth did not, therefore, constitute any obstacles for women's leader functions in the cult.

The Nærøyfjord – Njord's fjord

Njord, then, gave his name to the Nærøyfjord. The original name of the fjord was Njardarfjord which has gone through various sound changes to get its present name. Njord's home in the sky was called "Noatun". He is the god of weather and wind, sea and fire. Besides, he is so rich in goods and chattels that he can be linked to trade and markets. The fjord was the sea lane between east and west, also in prehistoric times. For people who lived inland, such as those who lived in the Voss area, the Nærøyfjord was their first encounter with the treacherous sea. They could not use this sea for travelling unless they were on good terms with the sea god, Njord. Consequently, it was to Njord they prayed when they came to the salt and wavy water. This was also the fjord that opened up their world to the main fjord and west across the ocean. The people from Voss named the Nærøyfjord after this sea god. Gods gave them protection.

Gudvangen – God's meadow

The archaeologist Anne Stine Ingstad makes a special reference to Gudvangen as an example that Njord could be a protector of markets. Ingstad is well known for her expertise in presenting arguments that North America was actually discovered by Vikings a thousand years ago. Gudvangen, the meadow of the god Njord, could have been the first "kaupang" (market town) in the Inner Sogn landscape, as well as an early "kaupang" in western Norway. Less important cult sites were often given names such as Horg, Lund or Vang. When the coastal people and the inland people met at Gudvangen to exchange commodities, they could make their sacrifices to the god Njord.

Ramsøy is not far from Gudvangen on the western side of the Nærøyfjord.

58

Fresvik – Frey's bay

Fresvik on a winter morning.

The place name Fresvik refers to the god Frey (Frøy in Norwegian). Frøysvik must have been the original name. There we also find other traces of a religious, pre-Christian community. The farm Hov ("hov" means place of worship) points directly back to the pre-Christian conception of the world and belief. At Hov in Fresvik there was in all likelihood a temple of worship. A "hov" was a major, public cult site where people congregated from a large geographical area.

Names based on Christian belief

This fjord has place names that are based on Christian belief. A case in point is Krossneset jutting out into the fjord. The point can be seen from a long distance. In the olden days there must have been a cross at this place. There were always crosses at places with names like Krossnes, Korssund, or Krosshaug. The cross most likely signified that all land behind it was Christian land. It could have been a spiritual struggle at this very fjord between the old belief and the belief in Jesus Christ. This cross could have been carved at Rønset in Hyllestad as was the case with so many other crosses, and transported onboard a ship at Otringsneset, then out the Åfjord, south through the strait of Tollesundet and then eastward on the main Sognefjord to the Nærøyfjord. Perhaps the idea behind it was to have a confrontation with Njord and Frey once and for all. This is how Krossneset got its name.

Few artists have been able to recreate the moment when the sun returns after long, dark winter months better than the Lærdal artist Hans Gjesme (1904-1994). Through his painting "The sun returns in the spring" he has caught the entire natural-mythical conception of sun and light found among the early Norwegians. The Gjesme gallery is located at Lærdalsøyri.

The days of the week in our international language

A lot of the Christianization policy in Norway a thousand years ago had to do with giving the pagan and Norse days of feast new content and new names. In some areas the names had become so established that it was impossible to get them changed. A case in point is the names of the week days. Our old Norse mythology belonged to a common European culture group. Many of the names of weekdays have the same origin in English and German.

The first day of the week is Sunday. In this case it is the worship of the sun – the great life-giving force – that has given its name to this day. Monday is the day of the moon, the pale orb that influences the water and everything that grows. Slaughtering animals when the moon is waning was considered a mortal sin. Tuesday has got its name after the Norse war god Tyr, son of Frigga and Odin (Woden). Tyr had only one hand, but he was still looked upon as the bravest of men. Wednesday was named after Odin, the All Father. He was the chief god of Norse mythology, above all other gods and men. Thursday derives its name after Thor, the god of thunder and strength, who was ranked after his father, Odin, but above all others. Thursday night at full moon was a time for witchcraft and sorcery. The only woman who has given her name to a week day is Frigga who has given name to Friday. Frigga was the foremost of all women. She was married to Odin and mother of Balder. The final day of the week was Saturday, named after the Roman god Saturn. In Norwegian, however, the day is called "lørdag" or "laurdag", which originally means the day of bathing and washing

The underworld and the fiddler Lisbet-Per

Stories of the little people in the underworld are called mythical legends. They are numerous both in the Inner Sogn area and elsewhere in the country. The wood nymphs were creatures from the underworld, living underground and in the mountains. They took over the operation of the mountain farms when the milk maids returned to the home farm in the autumn. The wood nymphs were strikingly beautiful women. They tempted men, causing erotic fantasies among them when they came secretly sneaking up in the middle of the night, even up to the bedposts. The only blemish the wood nymphs had was that they had cow tails. Sometimes the little people came forward, offering people something to drink. But even if the drink looked ever so fine, not a single drop must pass their lips. Then the outcome would be that they were finished as human beings.

People's notion of the little people was closely linked to their respect for nature. On some hilltops you could not cut the grass or remove foliage from the trees. The area was reserved for the underworld that people wanted to live in harmony with. If this harmony was broken, disaster would strike both animals and people. Sometimes people had built houses in such a way that the little people were disturbed. Then it could be impossible to prevent the barn roof from leaking. People then had only one option: Find another place to live.

The fiddler from Sogn who has most stories attached to his name was "Gudvangen" or Lisbet-Per from Gudvangen. He was a master fiddler, travelled extensively and had a vast knowledge and repertoire of tunes. "Gudvangen" was one of these master fiddlers about whom legends were freely spun in popular literature. He was allegedly on good terms with the little people, as was the case with many players. He knew "the witchcraft" in his music, writes Arne Bjørndal, our renowned folk music collector and expert. "Gudvangen" was able to make both living and dead dance to his fiddle.

The Norwegian writer Per Sivle wrote about "Gudvangen" in the mythical legend called "A Fiddler". The fiddler's name was Per, and his mother's name was Lisbet. Thus the name Lisbet-Per. Lisbet was a full-blooded traveller. Few people knew who the

The folk music originated in the natural surroundings and the mythical forces of nature.

The wood nymph ("huldra") was exceptionally beautiful. The only blemish she had was that she had a cow's tail.

Many ornamental objects had animals and dragons as motifs. This is the neck of a fiddle.

biological father was. Per himself expressed it like this, especially when he had emptied a glass or two: "If my mother was a sooty crow, then my father must have been a golden-feathered hawk."

Lisbet-Per was raised at Nesheim in the valley of Myrkdalen. He was clever and reliable, and not a single lamb was lost during the three summers he was a farmhand at Nesheim. The fourth summer Lisbet-Per was captured into the mountain by the wood nymphs. People tried to get him out by using soil from the churchyard, steel and family silver, but to no avail. On a Sunday morning in the autumn of the fourth year, Per came rushing in through the door, got hold of a knife and cut a cross on his left little finger and blood spurted out. Then a horrible scream was heard outside, but Per merely laughed, saying: "You did not get any man today, either, Guro Grebbe!"

Per said very little about his stay inside the mountain. He did not want to be a shepherd any longer, but he got himself work as a farmhand. The money he earned was spent on a fiddle. The master of the household mocked him: "you cannot even tune a fiddle". Per then sat down in the high chair, put the fiddle under his chin, and tunes poured out and were played in such a way that nobody had heard anything like it before. People laughed and cried, and when he really let go, the feet started to dance by themselves. Per soon became known as a master fiddler, not only at Voss, but also elsewhere in Hardanger and Sogn. He started travelling as a fiddler and made much money. He put the money aside, and people thought he was greedy. In addition to playing, he also started up as a peddler. Then he married a widow, and this is why he came to the farm of Gudvangen and became a wealthy man.

The river flowing past his farm has always been a good salmon river. On the opposite river bank is the farm of Ramsøy. Lisbet-Per lured the fish over to his side of the river by playing his fiddle. Consequently, very little salmon could be caught on the other side. But the Ramsøy farmer had the Book of Black Magic, so he called upon the Devil to play against Per. They sat on their river banks and played, Per and the Devil. For the first time in his life, Per was about to lose a contest. The fish was moving across to the other side. "Can I have a look at your fiddle", cried Per. The Devil came across the river with his instrument. Without the Devil noticing anything, Per managed to carve a cross on the Devil's fiddle. Afterwards Per played so well that three fat salmon jumped up on his river bank.

The troll was an ugly, hairy creature with a long nose. We can see trolls everywhere in nature, in the mountains and in primeval forests.

One Sunday Per walked about his farm, wanting to check the year's crop. All of a sudden he met a bridal procession of wood nymphs. They were on their way to church inside the mountain. Per at once threw a piece of iron over the bride. She remained standing while the rest of the party disappeared. Per then started to take off her silver jewellery and her clothes, leaving only her shift (undergarments), where her neckband was tied with a magnificent silver brooch. The wood nymph begged Per to give her back the silver, but Per was adamant. He stripped her of the shift and brooch as well. Suddenly, Per had no more power over the wood nymph, but before she disappeared into the mountain, she told Per that his offspring would suffer in body and soul in the ninth or tenth generation after him.

Per's last journey as a fiddler went to Hol in Hallingdal. There he played in such a way that not only people danced, but also stools, cups, and pots and pans. Even the house was lifted off its foundation so daybreak could be seen through the logs in the wall. Then tears rolled down his cheeks.

"Now Lisbet-Per has played well. Now other fiddlers can take over," he said. On his way home from Hol to Gudvangen, he broke through the ice on a mountain lake and drowned.

The regional costume from Sogn

Reconstructed woman's costume from the early 19th century. The baby is dressed in a baptismal dress from the early 20th century with a reconstructed baptismal cap from the 19th century.

The national costumes that we see today are based on a comprehensive national reconstruction work. It was through the national fervour after 1905 that these popular costumes were brought into the light again. Practically everybody had stopped using these costumes in the Inner Sogn area by then. The reconstruction work was based on older garments that were used for festivities and parties towards the end of the 18th century. This is what we today call "bunad" (national/regional costume). In the mid-1980s, the regional costume for Sogn was once more reconstructed. The men's costume was professionally reconstructed, whereas a women's costume from the early 19th century was reconstructed and taken into use in addition to the ordinary woman's regional costume.

The women's costume from Sogn is made of black wool material. It can be pleated, or closely let out and gathered at the waist. The skirt may have different borders at the bottom, but it is now usual to have a wide blue, red or green border with a zigzag upper edge. This zigzag pattern reflects the waves on the Sognefjord. The length of the skirt has followed the fashion trends over the years. The old folk costume in the Inner Sogn area had a somewhat shorter skirt than the one that has been reconstructed. The bodice is made of patterned brocade, bordered by black velvet bands. It is open at the front, and is held together by eyelet lacing. Various types of shirts are used. Today we see either a white linen shirt or a green silk shirt. The green colour indicates that the woman is married. The costume silver consists of a collar brooch, often with a pendant, and a bigger brooch further down. Black stockings and special "bunad" shoes were necessary accessories to the costume.

The women's costumes reflect moral conditions in the society and ranks among women. The costumes were meant to express differences between young and old, between married and unmarried. In the olden days unmarried women braided a woven ribbon into their hair, making a beautiful wreath around the head. According to tradition, married women were supposed to wear a wife's headdress made of a thin and white cotton material. In addition, married women were supposed to use a belt consisting of small, rectangular silver plates and silver belt buckle. The maiden belt was made of velvet with a silver buckle. These expressions concerning rank and status were not reflected in the men's costumes.

The men's costume from Sogn was reconstructed in 1986. The costume has a jacket of a coarse woollen cloth called "vadmål" in Norwegian (frieze). It can either be white or red with a high collar. The white jacket has dark blue borders, whereas the red one has

green. The breeches are made of black frieze or other cloths. The braces are made of woven red, white, or green wool. The waistcoat is also made of frieze. The shirt is made of white linen with different patterns of white-seam embroidery. The socks are white and hand-knitted in various patterns. A silk neckerchief is another accessory to the costume. The headgear is usually a round, bowl-shaped red cap or a peak cap made of wool with black velvet bands. The breeches buttons were made of cast brass or silver.

The writer Per Sivle

Per Sivle (1857-1904) is the writer of this landscape of national and international renown. He was born in Flåm, and in his restless childhood he lived at various places around Stalheim before he grew up like a son in the house at Brekke in the valley of Nærøydalen, with Brytteva and Bottolv.

The young Per was deeply impressed by the nature around him and created important literature where mountains and wild mountains always played a role as threatening backdrops. This is evident in his short story entitled "Only a dog" which is written as a childhood memory, placing it definitely among the gems of our national literature. Most people believe the writer when he says that this is a childhood memory, writes Bjarte Birkeland in his biography on Per Sivle. It is easy to corroborate the events. The Kvåle farm in the short story is Brekke, and the Jorbergnuten is Jordalsnuten. The topographical details are so accurate that we can easily recognize the landscape features between Gudvangen and Stalheim.

The old popular art of narration was held in high esteem at Vossestrand, and Sivle keeps up the tradition in a brilliant way. The collections of stories called "Vosse-stubba" and "Sagor" from 1887, "Nye Vossa-stubba" (1894) and "Sivle-stubba" (1895) represent some of the finest stories from everyday life ever written in Norwegian literature. A calm and personal style in these books has melted together with rural people's way of telling stories, which means that the oral character is preserved.

The life of the writer Per Sivle had peaks like the soaring mountains of Nærøydalen, but there were also sometimes downs when he lived in deep and sunless back valleys. Sivle understood the minds of children. Few other writers show like him that the child lives in the man. Sudden emotional changes, so characteristic of children, followed him throughout his life. Sivle shot himself with a pistol at a public bath in Oslo in 1904. On that day people cried at Flåm, Gudvangen, Nærøydalen, Oppheim and at Vossevangen. A Sivle monument, made by Lars Vetre, was unveiled at Voss in 1953.

Dialects

*Hege Strømme and
Dee Cunningham who
run the Stigen farm
lay the breakfast table
outdoors for their
guests.*

The Sogn dialect belongs to the branch that linguists call west Norwegian. Within the west Norwegian there are a number of clearly defined dialect areas. One of these is the Inner Sogn which is linked to Voss and Hardanger, and belongs to one of the most characteristic groups of western Norwegian dialects. The villages are located far from the coastal lanes and lean their backs to the mountains. For centuries they have been both administratively and ecclesiastically separated from the western villages. On the other hand, there has been extensive communication between Inner Sogn and Voss. This has drawn them in the same direction: Separated them from the areas further to the west, and made them more closely linked to one another.

The most characteristic feature of the Sogn dialect is that the "å" vowel sound (as in the English 'saw') is pronounced "ao" (as in the English dipthong in 'out'), as is the case also on Iceland and the Swedish region of Skåne. A case in point is the Norwegian noun for 'boat' "båt" (normally pronounced like 'bought'), but is pronounced like the English 'bout'. In the Inner Sogn area all verb infinitives end in –a, as in "kasta" (throw), "hoppa" (jump) and so on. The definite form of irregular feminine nouns ends in –i, as in "soli" (the sun), "døri" (the door), etc. The same thing applies to plural neuter nouns: "epli" (the apples), "husi" (the houses).

The strong goat cheese

Two types of goat cheese are produced in this area: white and brown. Both of these have a long tradition in Inner Sogn. The sweet brown cheese is something that few Norwegians can do without. The main principles for making cheese are practically the same in most areas, but there are still many local varieties.

Brown cheese from Underdal.

The village of Undredal has a strong and unbroken tradition for making this cheese. The milk comes from goats that are well adapted to the climate and the fjord landscape, where they climb the steep mountainside and feed on grass most of the year. Undredal was an isolated village until 1988. Previously you could only get there by boat or walk across the mountains. This isolation is one explanation why the people of Undredal have kept on with goat farming and cheese making. Its distinctive taste and local tradition has led to a great demand for this cheese, and it has a good reputation in the market. The demand is indeed greater than the supply, especially of the brown variety.

Underdal on the Aurlandsfjord.

The white goat cheese is made of raw, non-pasteurized milk. It is made from the curd in the goat milk, and is therefore the genuine goat cheese. The cheese must mature in special storage rooms before it is ready for consumption. Previously it was not common to add salt to the cheese. Instead, the crust was hardened by dipping the cheese in boiling whey. The practice of unsalted cheese has to do with the fact that the cheese was traditionally used with salt food such as bacon, herring and stew. Today both salted and unsalted white cheese is produced, depending upon demand. Every cheese wheel weighs about 2.5 kilos and is matured

from two to 12 months. The white cheese was traditionally used as a supplement to the daily fare at all meals.

The brown cheese is made of whey boiled for many hours according to local traditions. In Sogn this brown cheese is called "brimost". It is made from the by-product whey after the white cheese has been made. It takes 11 litres of goat milk to produce one kilo of goat cheese. The fresh whey is pumped into huge copper pans where it boils over open fire for eight to ten hours.

About 10% whole goat milk and two percent cream of cow milk are added to make the cheese less lean and not so dry in texture. The so-called Maillard reaction between the lactose sugar and the proteins in the whey mixture makes the cheese brown and gives it a caramel taste. After the boiling process, the "brimost", which contains most albumin (a protein), milk fat, and lactose sugar, is left to cool while being stirred until its texture is sufficiently firm. Then it is kneaded and pressed into square moulds. After one day, the cheese is solid enough to be taken out of the moulds, and, as no ripening is needed, is immediately ready for consumption. The cheese is a very stable and high-quality product. The cheese makers have developed a special wrapping which contains product information and it keeps well over long distances with big differences in temperatures. In other words, it is the ideal souvenir for tourists to take home.

"Gamalost" (literally: old cheese). Traditional Norwegian low-fat cheese made of sour skimmed milk, with a sharp, aromatic flavour.

In 1991, the cheese makers at Undredal were faced with a major challenge when the local Food Safety Authority demanded that they had to pasteurize the milk. One of the local producers, French-born Pascale Baudonnel, went to Surgères in France to get an education in cheese-making technology. She took up the fight with the authorities and demanded that all the small-scale farm cheese factories that wanted to should be allowed to use raw milk in their cheese production, as they do in France. Pascale and her husband now run a co-operative dairy along with two other families.

The goat cheese from Undredal is a local product, but it has become an international product as well through the organization called Ark of Taste which was established by the Slow Food Foundation for Biodiversity in 1996. Slow Food is a worldwide organization with its headquarters in Italy. Slow Food aims at supporting and promoting biological diversity by focusing on agricultural products linked to local nature and culture. One of Slow Food's many initiatives is the Ark of Taste, a catalogue of the most valuable products or species that need to be protected against biological and cultural homogenization resulting from globalization, for one thing. One of its objectives is to establish so-called Presidia for products they want to promote and support. In the summer of 2005, Slow Food decided to establish the first Norwegian Presidium. This honour was awarded to the Undredal cheese as a representative for "Brimost from Sogn".

"Smalahove" (sheep's head)

White dots of sheep on green hillsides in spring. In the summer they graze on lush mountain pastures.

The Inner Sogn area and Voss both belong to the geographical cultural area where the fleece and skin of sheep heads were torched. Further west along the coast, the heads were skinned. It is the people of Voss who have made an industry out of this common denominator of our cultural area. They have developed this traditional dish into something out of this world. Voss is always close to the people of Inner Sogn, and maybe a sense of community linked to food and drink is the closest you can get to brotherhood and sisterhood. After the tunnel revolution was carried out in Inner Sogn, Voss has gradually become a cultural disseminator, spreading its influence over the villages of Sogn.

The eating of sheep's head is a ceremony that must date back to the Viking Age. New eaters of "smalahove" must learn that the taste varies from one part of the head to another. The fat meat around the ears has one taste, the fat around the eye another, whereas the meat on the cheek bones tastes differently again.

– All senses must be sharpened and concentrated on the one and only essential matter: enjoying the food, writes the author and playwright Norvald Tveit in his book "Smalahove", adding that the meal should be an orgy, but an orgy at slow speed.

Scorching sheep heads and organizing parties based on this tasty dish has become an industry at Voss.

Smoked salmon

The river of Lærdalsøyri has been called the queen among Norwegian salmon rivers. British lords came here to fish salmon that they smoked and cured and brought back home.

More than a century ago, English lords came to the Lærdalselva river to fish salmon. According to local yarns, the river was so full of fish that if you wanted salmon for dinner, you only had to go down to the river bank and pick one up. The lords used local "smokers" from Lærdal to cure the salmon to make it keep and be tasty after the long journey back to Britain. In the same way that the lords had their salmon cured in the 19th century, you get it in the shop today, completely free of any artificial additives.

Kjell Grøtte established the company "Sognefjord Gourmet", formerly called "Lærdalsmat", and one of their main products is smoked salmon. The Lærdalselvi river, sometimes called the queen of salmon rivers in Norway, has rich and long-established traditions. This does not only apply to fly tying, but also to food. The recipes for this special smoked salmon have been found among the fishing communities along the river. Producing smoked salmon in this way has become a niche product. Elsewhere the production of smoked salmon has become industrialized, and there are very few traditional smokehouses left. The salmon is delivered to shops and supermarkets, restaurants and hotels in Norway, but "Sognefjord Gourmet", which is located at Årdal, aims at exporting salmon to exclusive markets abroad.

In order to ensure optimal quality, new technology must necessarily be taken into use. Sometimes new knowledge is introduced from abroad. This is the case with herb-smoked salmon which has been developed in connection with an export initiative in Asia. Asians prefer a somewhat less salty taste than we are used to in Norway. The herb-smoked salmon has a more harmonious and well-balanced taste of fish, smoke, salt and herbs. Quality is also paramount in their production of other commodities, such as gravlax (dry-cured salmon marinated in herbs). These recipes are also from the valley of Lærdalsdalen where there are long traditions of curing salmon in this way. This very special process most likely has roots back to the Viking Age.

Smoking salmon with juniper underneath.

The Aurland moccasin

The Aurland shoe or moccasin has been produced in Aurland for many generations. The original Aurland shoe had laces, but today it is produced as a moccasin. The production has been carried out in small-scale factories or as one-man enterprises. In the golden age of the Aurland shoe, about 90 persons were employed in shoe production, and these shoemaker shops represented the best sources of tax revenue for the local authorities.

As early as about 1880, Vebjørn Sjursen Vangen and Andreas Vangen started the first production of Aurland shoes for sale. They became so popular that they were even exhibited at the Chicago World Fair in 1893. However, it was not until Nils Tveranger from Solund in 1908 established a factory production of a shoe type that resembled the original Aurland shoe that the shoe production became an important industry. These shoes had lacing with a burned pattern on top of the shoe itself. The shoe was also exhibited at the Bergen Fair in 1910, and was awarded a prize.

Tveranger's shoes were patented under the name "The National Shoe". Later on, Gustav Nesbø and Kristian Ohnstad took up the production of this "national shoe". In 1935, Tveranger designed the Aurland shoe as we know it today. The Aurland shoe was also exported to the USA and the other Nordic countries. In Denmark the shoe was called "Norwegian cottage shoe". It became fashionable to insert a small ten-øre coin in between the bands of leather on top. The small coin was visible, and in a way it also tied bands between young people, within a modern fashion.

The production of the shoe reached its peak in the 1950s and the 1960s. 18 companies produced the Aurland shoe in the 20th century, most of these in Aurland, but also a few in Flåm. The sole producer since the early 1970s has been the Aurland Shoe Factory with about six employees. Today the shoe is made in three colours: light natural leather, black and burgundy.

Voluspå

In the pre-Christian mythology women occupied a central position. They were prophetesses or priestesses who could voice prophecies on future events and interpret the vision for the future. One of the oldest and most beautiful poems in the European literature from pre-Christian times is called "Voluspå". In the words of the sibyl (prophetess), we see the landscape around the Nærøyfjord ahead of us, after the earth has sunk into the sea.

She sees the Earth
Rising a second time
From the ocean
Once again clad in green.
Water falls
Eagle soars
Catching fish
In the mountains

This is the Nærøyfjord, our Norwegian fjord. Water falls, the eagle soars. "Solaløysa" is once more clad in green after the long winter months.

FACTS AND FIGURES

Inscribed in the UNESCO World Heritage List: 2005
Protected area: 709 square kilometres
Municipalities concerned: Aurland, Lærdal and Vik in the Sogn
                                               og Fjordane county, Voss in the
                                               Hordaland county

Stops (quays):   Dyrdal, Styvi, Tufto, Bakka,
                                               Bleiklindneset, Gudvangen
Permanent residents (2006):   Gudvangen incl. Nærøydalen about
                                               70, Bakka 13, Tufto 5,
                                               Dyrdal 0, Styvi 2
Number of tourists (2005):   313 350 (of these about 300 000 in
                                               summer, about 13 500 in winter)

Number of overnight visitors
(Aurland and Lærdalin 2005):   about 230 000
Number of cruise ships (Gudvangen 2005):   59
Number of car ferry routes: 1 in summer
Number of boat routes: 3 in summer, 1 in winter

Geography

Length of fjord:	17 kilometres
Narrowest point:	The strait of Bakkasundet – 250 metres
Deepest point:	376 metres at Beitelen
Shallowest point:	The strait of Bakkasundet – 10 metres
Biggest difference between high and low tide:	1.4 metres
Highest mountain around the Nærøyfjord:	Bakkanosi – 1389 metres
Highest altitude difference between fjord bottom and mountain top:	about 2000 metres
Largest glacier:	Fresvikbreen – 15 square kilometres
Number of waterfalls:	25
Highest free drop of waterfall:	Kjelfossen – 200 metres

Climate Aurlandsvangen

Average air temperature:	January -4°C, July 14.8°C
Average annual precipitation:	685 millimetres
Month with the highest precipitation:	October
Month with the lowest precipitation:	April
	(readings for the period 1961-90)

The temperature in the Nærøyfjord may vary from 0 to 20°C. When the snow melts in spring, the salinity in the water is reduced. This surface water warms up to about 20 - 22°C in the summer, and further down the water is colder and saltier. In the winter it is the other way around with more salt water in the surface layer because there is less melting water. Consequently, the upper layer is very cold, and deeper down in the fjord the water gets gradually warmer. Every winter the fjord freezes over from Gudvangen and frequently all the way out to the strait of Styvisundet.

Literature:
Askeland, Jan og Halvdan Ljøsne 2000. Knut Rumohr. Bergen.

Benedictow, Ole Jørgen 1999.
«Hedendom – kristendom – statsrett». I: Jan-Erik Ebbestad Hansen
(red). Norsk tro og tanke 1000 – 1940. Oslo.

Birkeland, Bjarte 1962. Per Sivle. Oslo.

Bjørkum, Anders mfl. (red) 1964.

Sogn heime og ute. Oslo.

Bondevik, Kjell 1977.

Jordbruket i norsk folketru. Oslo.

Borgen, Johan 1980. Natt og dag. Oslo/Gjøvik.

Bøthun, Per H 1965. Leikanger Bygdebok. Leikanger.

Christensen, Arne Emil 1970. «Isbåtene i Sogn».
I: Sjøfartshistorisk Årbok 1971. Bergen.

Eide, Ove m.fl (red) 1999. Vestland,Vestland. Oslo.

Fossnes, Heidi 1993. Norges bunader og samiske folkedrakter. Oslo.

Førsund, Finn Borgen 1998. Dampen og kaia. Førde.

Holmsen, Andreas 1971. Norges historie. Oslo/Bergen/Tromsø.

Ingstad, Anne Stine 1992. «Osebergdronningen – hvem var hun?»
I: Arne Emil Christensen. Osebergdronningens grav. Oslo

Marschall, Birgit 1991. Reisen und Regieren. Bremerhaven/Hamburg.

Ohlmarks, Ove 1995. Fornnordisk Lexikon. Stockholm.

Olsen, Magnus 1967: «Ættegård og helligdom».
I: Andreas Holmsen. Rikssamling og kristendom. Oslo

Sigurdsson, Jon Vidar 1999. Norsk historie 800-1300. Oslo.

Svendsen, Morten (red) mfl. 2004. Hans Gjesme. Leikanger.

Thue, Johs.B. 1993. Brev til Ingebjørg den Fagre av Sogn. Leikanger.

Torvanger, Magnus Helge 2000. 101 Fjordabåtar. Førde.

Tveit, Norvald [1985] 1994. Smalahove. Oslo.

Aall, Hans 1937.

Norske Bygder. Bind IV. Sogn. Bergen

Aaraas, M. H. mfl. 2000. På kyrkjeferd i Sogn og Fjordane. Førde.

Nettbaserte artiklar frå Fylkesarkivet i Sogn og Fjordane og NRK Sogn
og Fjordane.

Photo:
Alf T. Engeset 68, Einar S. Husabø 14, Erik Hoel 35, Geir Flatabø
42b, Gjesmesamlinga 61, Helge Sunde 4, 8, 9, 10, 13, 17, 19, 22, 23a,
23b, 25, 28, 30, 36b, 37, 38, 39, 42a, 43a, 43b, 49, 56, 59, 64, 66b, 70,
72, 73b, 78, 82, 84, Ivar Løne 77, Kjersti Isdal 65, 66a, 67, Leif-Arne
Furevik 45, Leiv Bergum 32, Noralv Distad 46, Oddleiv Apneseth 54a,
54b, Oddmund Lunde 15, 16a, 16b, 47, 55, Oscar Andersen 79, Pascale
Baudonnel 73a, 74, 75, Roar W. Vangsnes 69, Sarah J. Hails 26, Simone
Stibbe 29, 60. 63, 81, Svein Ulvund 33, Svenn Vegard Lunde 40, Terje
Eggum 7, 21, 36a, UiB Billedsamlingen (KnudKnudsen) 48, 52, Sogn
Folkemuseum (Ø. Færøyvik) 27.

Cover photo: HELGE SUNDE
English translation: JAN TALSETHAGEN
Graphic design: SILJE NES/ ARNE BARLINDHAUG ELLINGSEN
Print: PDC TANGEN 2006

ISBN (norsk utgåve) 82-7959-074-9
ISBN (English edition) 82-7959-075-7